THE Ballad OF Morgowr

Written and illustrated by
JUDY SCRIMSHAW

A catalogue record for this book is available from the British Library.

ISBN 978-0-9932870-1-5 Paperback Edition.

Published by Granny Moff Books.

For more copies of this book, please email judy@grannymoff.com.

Designed and set by John Greenwood. www.artdesk.uk, email john@artdesk.uk.

Printed by ARRC Print Ltd.
ARRC Studio No46, Crellow Fields, Stithians, Truro, Cornwall, TR3 7RE. e: info@arrcprint.co.uk.

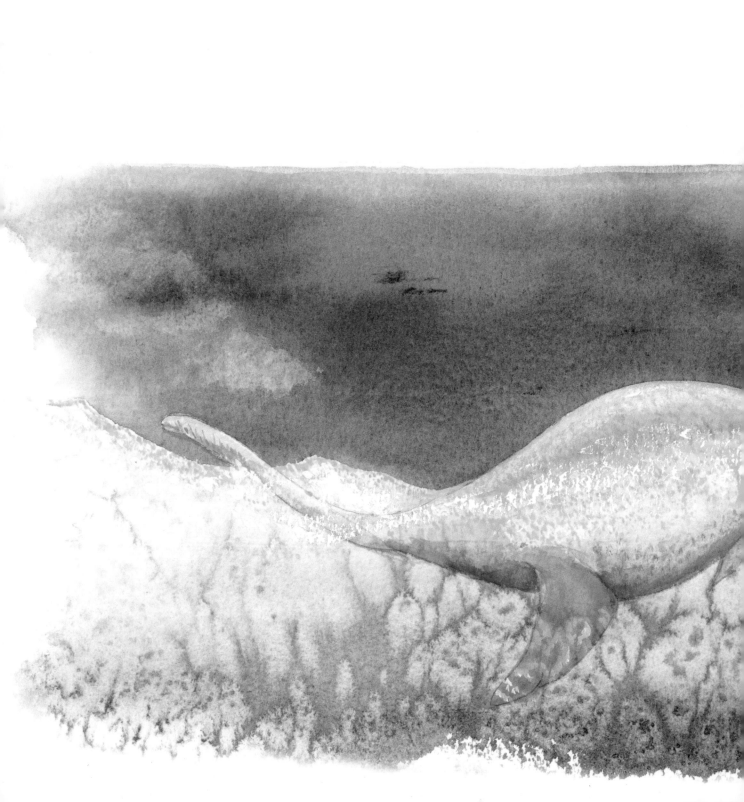

for
James
Lucas, Theo Bear,
William, Oliver, Amelie,
Willie and Mary

'Sea Giant' in the ancient
Cornish language is Morgowr
and so I have been named for years,
a creature of great power.

Let me tell you now my story
of how I came to be
living in the Helford River,
Falmouth Bay and Cornish Sea.

It was in salty waters
where Plesiosaurs began,
in the Jurassic period
before the world of man.

My ancient relatives lived here
with nothing much to fear,
minding their own business
for years and years and years.

Until in late Cretaceous time
at nightime they did view
a comet (or an asteroid)
towards their world it flew...

to crash with such explosion
which had nowhere else to go
but round the world at high speed
– CATACLYSMIC INFERNO!

Poor Cretaceous dinosaurs
had no chance to escape.
The world became an oven;
in a firestorm flash they baked.

The only creatures to survive
the fire and glowing heat
hid underground, or dived below
the sea in their retreat.

Gigantic dinos ran and fell
with such a mighty crash.
Extinction took a moment -
it was over in a flash.

When this giant rock struck earth
with deafening roar and glow,
we survived that deadly blast
by diving far below.

We swam down to a hiding place
some 20,000 feet;
an Atlantic ocean trench, now called
the Puerto Rico Deep.

The fallout blotted out the sun
green plants no longer grew.
For months it was forever dark,
no sunlight filtered through.

When the last meat-eating dinos
on dead vegesaurs had fed,
with nothing left but hard, dry, bones -
they too all fell down dead.

Plesiosaurs continued living
way down in briny seas,
surviving in the dark down there,
just surfacing to breathe.

Having outlived land dinosaurs
down in the oceans deep,
we spent much of our time eating,
or simply fast asleep.

It was not quite as scary
living there as you might think;
we were entertained by fish
lit up with lights that blinked...

and flashed in wondrous colours
of every type and hue -
fluorescent greens and yellows,
red, orange, pink and blue.

Into this world of weird fish
and creatures I was born.
As I grew I longed to visit
foreign seas and waters warm...

...where the world was now a different place,
new plants were quite a feature.
Birds and mammals lived, rather
than prehistoric creatures.

Those dinosaurs had disappeared
with fossils left behind;
a new animal took their place,
a rascal named mankind.

As man evolved, most creatures
he hunted; we did fear
we'd be no exception,
that fact seemed very clear.

Yet I wished to see this world,
leave the Rico Trench behind,
explore European waters
and even see mankind.

My mother was insistent
and so, indeed, was Dad,
that being seen by human kind
was very, VERY bad.

"To keep yourself quite safe, my dear,"
said Mother with a wink,
"be invisible to men -
they'll think you are extinct!"

So, I left the cold, dark ocean floor
and travelled all alone
to shallow seas, in which I could
explore all on my own...

...to a home in warmer waters
in the Gulf Stream; I can boast
of good living and fine fishing
in the Southern Cornish Coast.

In Falmouth Bay and River
of the Helford I do dwell.
For centuries I hid myself
and did it very well...

...or so I thought! Until one day
I had become too lazy,
so did not spy the fishing boat
in misty morn so hazy.

And yes, I did get caught by nets
in Eighteen Seventy Six.
I thought my time was really up
in such a dreadful fix.

With no way out of it, I stuck
my head up from the sea.
To my surprise, those fisherman
were more afraid of me!

Oh, please don't eat us!" cried the men
whilst hiding in the keel;
"Don't worry" I said gently,
"I prefer a fishy meal."

Although those lads were most polite
and wished for me to stay
to talk some more, I said "Good bye"
and carried on my way.

Well, humans did not seem at all
as bad as I've been told;
they had not tried to hunt me,
nor were they bad and bold.

Perhaps I'd be less careful
to hide myself from view,
sometimes to peep at tourist folk
or smile at a ship's crew.

Oh deary me! It started then,
you've guessed it, I was spied.
A Falmouth Packet's article
began to hue and cry.

Now boat trips filled with Emmets
visit estuary and creeks,
they chug from Falmouth Bay along
the Helford towards Gweek.

Some call a tourist 'Emmet'
believing it to be
a Cornish word meaning an 'ant'
but it's incorrect you see...

...because there's not a single word
in the Cornish dictionary
for 'ant'! Yet I've heard it used
around the West Country.

They're told of Morgowr sightings
right back to days gone past -
of a huge sea monster
by fishermen caught fast.

Some tell I have a beak-like head,
a dog, some others say,
but I don't crow, nor do I bark
when fishing Falmouth Bay.

Also I'm called a seal,
I can't think how they dare.
I don't look like one at all,
however huge and rare.

I've had my photograph in print
and, though I point no blame,
I'd like to keep my secrecy,
I do not relish fame.

The photos in the "Packet" news
were never very clear.
"I bet they are a hoax" I've heard
them often jeer.

But truth be told 'twas me who made
those photos very messy.
I was taught this brilliant trick
by Scottish cousin Nessy.

When surfacing to breathe I'd suck
some water up my nose;
it made me sneeze, the messy mist
hid me when I arose!

I decided to be careful
in the future, so I would
not count on every human
being kind to me, or good.

I tried again so very hard,
to hide myself away
from the sight of people,
underwater every day.

Unfortunately one foggy night
when the time was getting late,
I was engrossed in hunting eels
so made a huge mistake.

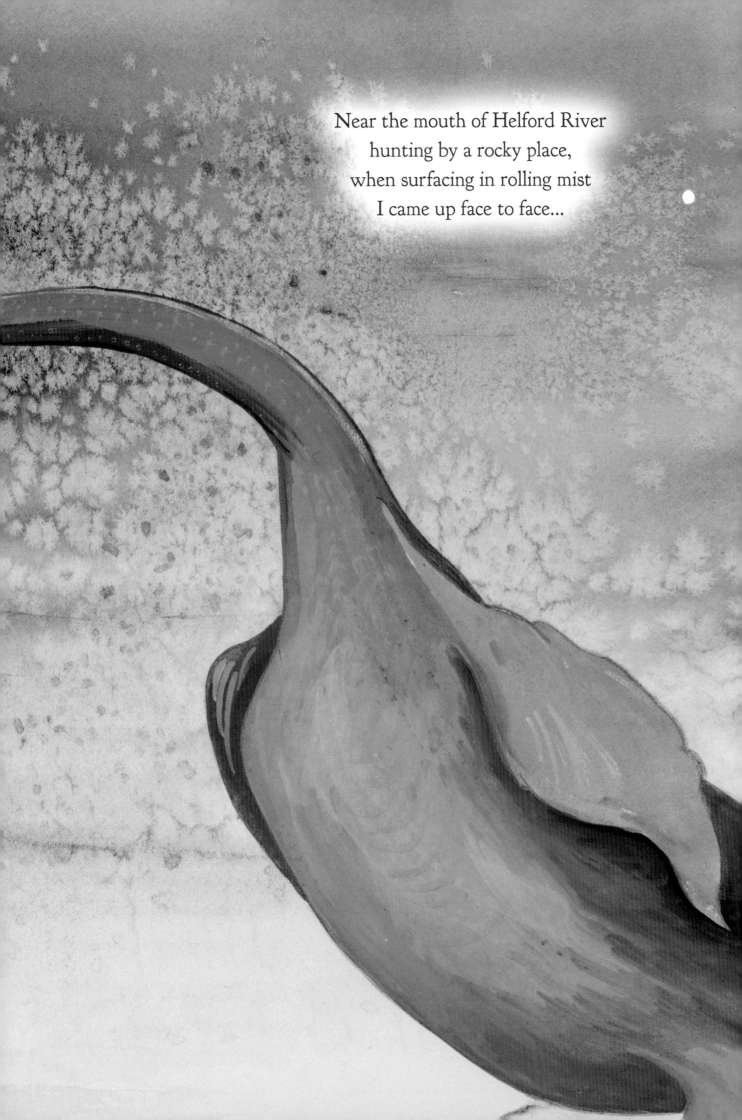

Near the mouth of Helford River
hunting by a rocky place,
when surfacing in rolling mist
I came up face to face...

...with a crew of three large tourists
from upcountry. They'd got lost
in the thick sea fog and worried
that this delay would cost...

...them lots of time and money
for they'd caught few fish to sell.
But as soon as they had seen me
all the crew began to yell:

"We can make a fortune
if we catch this giant beast.
How much do you think she's worth?
A million quid at least!"

"Let's chase this famous monster
keeping close upon her trail.
Can you see her through this sea fret?
Yes, there's her pointy tail."

So, with their motor roaring
they did nearer get and came
close up right behind me,
this was not a pleasant game.

Swimming as fast as ever
I could against the tide,
at a part of the River
where the estuary was wide.

I swam over the oyster beds
heading towards Gweek.
Their boat was so near to me
I could clearly hear them speak...

...through fog so thick; nearby I heard
cows chewing on the cud.
I tried to lose the men but
they were out to get my blood.

Mists swirling up rose thick and high
in a creek nearby.
Could I hide within it
while those rascals passed me by?

If they ignored me and went on
my plan would be perfection;
yet it went all wrong because
they took the same direction.

"I'm trapped", I thought, "where can I hide?
They'll find me in this creek.
This is a serious matter,
it's no game of hide and seek."

They meant to capture me, and then
sell me for lots of money.
I was not happy with this thought,
it was not very funny.

With mighty effort up the creek
I swam and then did leap
onto the shore - up , up the hill
whose path was mighty steep.

The trees they seem to bow and bend
trying to cover me,
to hide me from those fishermen
who chased me from the sea.

A distant memory did try
to surface in my mind,
while through the darkly wooded path
I slipped and jerked and climbed.

If only I could remember
what my Mother taught to me.
I stopped to catch my breath beneath
an ancient, gnarled oak tree.

My scaly legs were made to swim
not climb on mud and rock.
I puffed and panted on, at last
I made it to the top...

...into a meadow clear and bright
above the dark creek's tide.
I looked around, but could not find
a decent place to hide.

I crouched beside a Cornish hedge,
no cover could I find
and tried to calm my rising fear
hoping to clear my mind.

I searched around and spied nearby,
outbuildings of a farm,
but they were now in ruins -
an old cow shed and a barn.

No place to hide me from their view;
those fisherman were bound
to tie me up with chains and ropes
as soon as I was found.

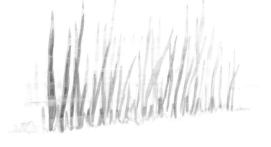

A memory from distant past:
my Mother once had told
of ancient powers to change our form
if we would be so bold.

Giant creatures from the sea
(of legend, myth and fable)
can change their form to Earth's hard rock,
by magic we are able.

Certain things must be just so,
the moon quite full and bright;
a mist must lay upon the sea
to make the spell just right.

A simple word must then be said
out loud in ancient tongue
of Cornish language, which I'd learnt
when I was very young.

What was that word? I wish I knew,
my heart was full of fear.
The voices of those nasty guys
were getting very near.

The men were coming closer still,
they'd capture me for sure;
move me around aquariums
to live forever more.

"The men, they come" I gasped, "the men"
"Oh deary, deary me!"
And so my fate seemed written
as no time was left to flee.

Through rising mists the full moon shone,
made me forget my fear.
Softly, as her light shone down
my mind became quite clear.

Saying 'men' made me remember
what in Cornish it does mean.
To weave the spell I must speak out
before I could be seen.

In Cornish the word 'men' or 'mean'
is a noun meaning a stone.
Whereas 'menha' is the verb
'petrify': 'turn to stone'.

If I could only change to rock.
"Menha!" I cried in panic.
Then to my surprise and glee
my body turned to granite!

From magic of that misty moon
my grey skin caught the light,
turning to granite stone so cold
with micah flashing bright.

Stiff hairs along my neck and back
receded to form bumps.
My sleek, smooth head turned into
one enormous lump.

My body sunk into the soil,
most of it deep beneath;
head and neck stood proud and strong
with legs far underneath.

The bad guys had almost reached
the meadow by the wood.
Could my transformation
be complete and any good?

In that magical old language
I had somehow changed to stone;
that incantation 'menha'
had petrified my bones!

A Friesian cow, called Maisey, watched
my change with huge surprise.
Walking in front of my stone self
she fixed me with brown eyes...

...and with a wink she lowered down
her head, rubbed neck and most
of her warm back against myself,
her brand new scratching post!

"A brilliant camouflage!" I thought
"what about my back and rump
which used to rise above the waves
as grey sea-monster humps?"

They'd turned to stone!
I had no fears -
it looked as if the rounded rocks
had been here years and years and years!

It fooled those nasty hunters,
the ones who wished to do me wrong,
who hunted for me high and low
and wondered where I'd gone.

"Where is she?" I heard one cry.
They gathered up their nets and ropes.
All were in a filthy mood
as gone were money-making hopes.

"We'd better now be getting back,
don't want to miss the tide.
If it goes out, the boat be stuck.
We'll end up high and dry."

So down they sped and at the shore
they waded out and stuck
fast in the mud, dark slimy stuff -
disgusting, stinky muck!

This mud was made of rotting stuff,
of shellfish dead and smelly:
oysters, cockles, mussels too,
into a black mud jelly.

They climbed out of their gumboots
and squelched back to their boat,
all had boring hours to wait
'til high tide made them float.

Eventually they roared away
without their pairs of wellies.
Muddy, wet, so cold and stiff
with grumbling, hungry bellies.

No longer were there sightings
around the Cornish coast;
no stories or photographs
for newspapers to boast.

Was Morgowr's destiny to be
a lifeless lump of stone,
an itching block for bovine friends,
to stand there all alone?

Alone to wait for someone else
to speak an incantation,
to use two special Cornish words
to make the right reaction.

A human child must undo
the spell and make things right.
It had to be in summertime
in misty, full moonlight.

And so for years and years I stood,
a granite standing stone;
while daisies nodded at my base,
I waited all alone.

Seasons and years went by,
my home was changed by man.
The ruined buildings were rebuilt
with landscaped garden plan...

...of such a pretty garden
packed with flowers and dainty trees,
the place was full of birdsong
while leaves whispered in the breeze.

At last my form was hidden
by shrubs, trees and flowers;
bluebells surrounded me
underneath the leafy bowers.

I slept in peace, quite comatosed
inside the solid rock,
for many years until one day
a visitor did knock...

...upon my stone, "I know you're there",
a young voice spoke to me.
"I can see through your disguise,
giant creature of the sea."

He kept on gently tapping,
asking me to come and play.
"I wonder if you move at night?"
he said, "You don't by day."

I could not clearly hear him,
being spellbound, yet it seemed
that something stirred inside me,
like waking from a dream.

"I'll return here tonight,
I'm staying with my Gran
in that converted barn, nearby."
And with that, off he ran.

That night was full of scented flowers,
of roses in full bloom,
whose colours faded in the light
of golden-haloed moon.

The small boy crept out of the barn,
he should have been in bed,
but moonlight drew him to the rock
he thought looked like a head.

A paintbox, brush and water jar
he held, then reached up high
to carefully paint several teeth
and magical blue eyes.

Standing back to view his work,
the scene lit by the moon,
two words repeated in his head
like a familiar tune.

Where they had come from he knew not,
but did not hesitate
to repeat them to my granite self
then step back to await.

"Morgowr" J whispered to me
"Dasvewa" which means
in Cornish to "live again":
once more I would be seen.

Alive again! To swim once more
with joy into the sea.
I did not believe my luck,
could this really be?

I said many a 'thank you'
to the little lad.
He was overjoyed to see
me so very glad.

The warmth spread through my body
from my head right down my side.
"Hey! Jump aboard, hold on tight,
I'll take you for a ride."

He said, "I'll grab my wetsuit,
as I'm sure you will agree,
with pyjamas wet and clingy,
I'll feel frozen in the sea."

I returned and clambered up my back.
Around me earth did boil.
Suddenly I sprang right out
of Mother Nature's soil...

...down the hill, all helter-skelter
to splash into the waves.
The little lad clung round my neck
which really was quite brave.

The buzz of freedom was intense,
my soul quite full of joy.
I hoped this feeling was now shared
with my new friend, the boy.

We surged out of the River
with an enormous wake
which seemed to glow and be on fire,
but this was really fake...

...for tiny plankton were splashed up
into the briny waves.
Their weird glow reminded me
of fish in former days...

...and my family, deep down below
so many miles away.
I wondered were they well?
If I'd see them all one day?

"I'd send them all a message",
speaking what was on my mind.
"I'll swim out along the coast
in order there to find..."

"...a wondering sea creature -
dolphin, whale or Basking shark.
So look for phosphorescence
glowing brightly in the dark."

We journeyed to the Manacles
right beside the Bell;
a large shark was cruising,
but what type we could not tell.

Understandably the young boy
was nervous in the dark.
Could we see what fish this was?
Perhaps a GREAT WHITE SHARK!

"Don't worry," I said cheerily
"I'm sure you needn't fear.
Great whites don't swim these waters
at any time of year."

"But, to keep you happy,
climb aboard the 'Bell'.
Don't worry if she sings out,
that's how ships can tell..."

"...they are near a rocky danger
(you can't see when you're on deck).
Those needle rocks below us
have claimed no end of wrecks."

The old bell, within the buoy
in rough seas loudly rings,
warning ships about the rocks
she mournfully does sing.

As J clambered up the buoy
I had an empty feel,
so dived below to fill my tum
with tasty conger eel.

All alone now, J noticed
a huge dorsal fin slide near
and yes, another one behind
which added to his fear.

The first shark swam right to him.
He hoped it would pass by,
but it was obviously watching him
with both its dull black eyes.

An enormous mouth gaped open -
he was about to scream.
Was this real, or maybe just
a nightmare of a dream?

"Morgowr, rescue me!" he yelled.
I heard the muffled cry
whilst swimming through the jagged rocks
in a fast, shallow dive.

I surfaced. He was mistaken
the second fin was just a tail.
"Hey!" this is a nice friendly shark,
no need to look so pale!"

"Basking Sharks gather here
with Summer plankton bloom.
They love to feed around the Bell
and listen to her tune."

They have no teeth but feed on
plankton during the day,
in warm Cornish waters
around the month of May.

Plankton drift along the surface
of the ocean in a group:
tiny plants and animals
make a delicious soup!

J peered through the water,
the shark came very near.
He stretched his hand to touch her,
he'd overcome his fear.

I said, "She's friendly but don't stroke,
you think she's smooth? You're wrong.
Her skin's like coarse sandpaper
and she's thirty two feet long!"

Then Morgowr spoke to the shark
"Please do me a great favour?
I apologise if you think this
is very strange behaviour."

"I'm worried that my family
in Rico Trench may fear
that I am dead and gone;
no one's seen me for years."

"Please let the other Plesiosaurs know
that I have been in hiding,
but now can roam free, fit and well.
Can you pass on these tidings?"

"Perhaps you may travel in
the direction of their home,
but I don't wish to put you out
in where you wish to roam."

"I'm heading off due North", she said
"with friends and there will I,
hopefully find lots of food
round the Isles of Mull and Skye."

The Basking Shark continued,
"But I'm bound to see some whales
who sing to one another
about exciting tales..."

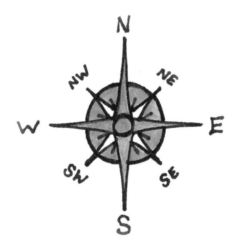

"so your message then will travel
round the ocean and the sea,
eventually it's bound to reach
your Plesiosaur family."

Skye

Mull

"How brilliant!" cried Morgowr,
"we wish you well upon your way!"
With that the boy climbed back on
and we swam to Falmouth Bay

where I enjoyed more food,
a mouthful of eels.
While J sat on some rocks
accompanied by seals.

As moonlight lit the bay
a rip current made a band
of silver in the dark blue sea
around a steep headland.

Along this tide was cruising
a Bull shark - fearsome beast -
hungry and unhappy,
what he needed was a feast.

It was highly unusual
for such a shark to be
swimming in these temperatures
of such a cool sea.

This great big fish swam up to me
and started to complain,
about our Cornish waters.
He really was a pain!

"I've been told your summertime
this year was good and hot,
so I travelled the Atlantic
to find this lovely spot..."

"...only to find the water here
for me is far too cold.
I can't find enough to eat,
perhaps I'm getting old!"

I expect you're wondering why
I talked to the shark that night
and worry that it would give
the little boy a fright.

You're right! As we were talking
the boy began to feel
quite nervous, especially when
he mentioned about meals.

"I don't trust that hungry shark."
he whispered, "Won't he bite?"
His ginormous mouth is full
of teeth so sharp and white."

Turning my head, I smiled at him
"There's no way he'll attack.
You're safe as long as you get up,
climb upon my back."

The shark continued moaning
about baited hooks which dangle
from fishing boats, thus he'd swim back
to the Bermuda Triangle.

So into the Atlantic
he swam off due Sou'-West.
We waved him off, though both agreed
he was a scary pest.

I was surprised to see the dawn,
this night had seemed so fleeting.
I must return the lad back home,
few hours were left for sleeping.

As we swam back up the River
in my mouth was something cold
and hard that stuck between my teeth -
a coin, and made of gold!

Perhaps the eel had swallowed it
when hiding in a wreck.
I gave it as a parting gift to J,
clinging round my neck.

He gave me a fond farewell hug
and thanked me for the treasure.
I said I was delighted,
it had been a real pleasure.

Eventually J fell asleep
in his little bed,
with seals, sharks and Plesiosaurs
still racing in his head.

I slipped into the garden,
waiting for the moon
to set because I knew that
I'd petrify quite soon because...

Satellites and radar give
my whereabouts away.
So now I am forced to hide
from sight, by night and day.

Even if you are a local
or an 'Aug' on holiday,
I doubt if you will see me
in the River or the Bay.

Unless it is in a moonlit night
when Banshee owls do shriek,
I change my form and slide down
the footpath to the creek.

To my surprise I've found that I
can change from stone at will,
so when I'm very hungry
I can hunt eels to my fill.

Now when my tummy's full of eel
I'll swim back up the River
on a high tide from the creek
then up the hill to slither...

...to become stone once again,
I really do not mind.
Perhaps one day you'll find me
and I hope you'll be so kind...

...to keep my strange location
a secret between us
or people will come in thousands
by helicopter, car or bus.

So, thank you all for listening.
Hope you haven't found it boring.
Please do add to my story
by making your own drawing.

Thank you,
love from

Morgowr
xXx

The End

...of this tail!

Many thanks to...

Allen Scrimshaw

All my family

Cornish Quest

Bernard Deacon - Hon. Research fellow and
Pol Hodge - education officer of Maga, the Cornish Language Partnership

Elizabeth Rapp - Poet

John Greenwood - Book Design Consultant

Paul Lewin - Artist

Ryya Bread - Assistant Editor

Clare Scrimshaw - Assistant Editor

Simon Cook - Photographer

Simon Williams - Artist

Susan Hillier - Artist

Redruth Reference Library

Rose Boothby - Proof Reader

Sue Sidery - Proof Reader

The Falmouth Packet

The Princessa

and of course, Morgowr!

Lands End

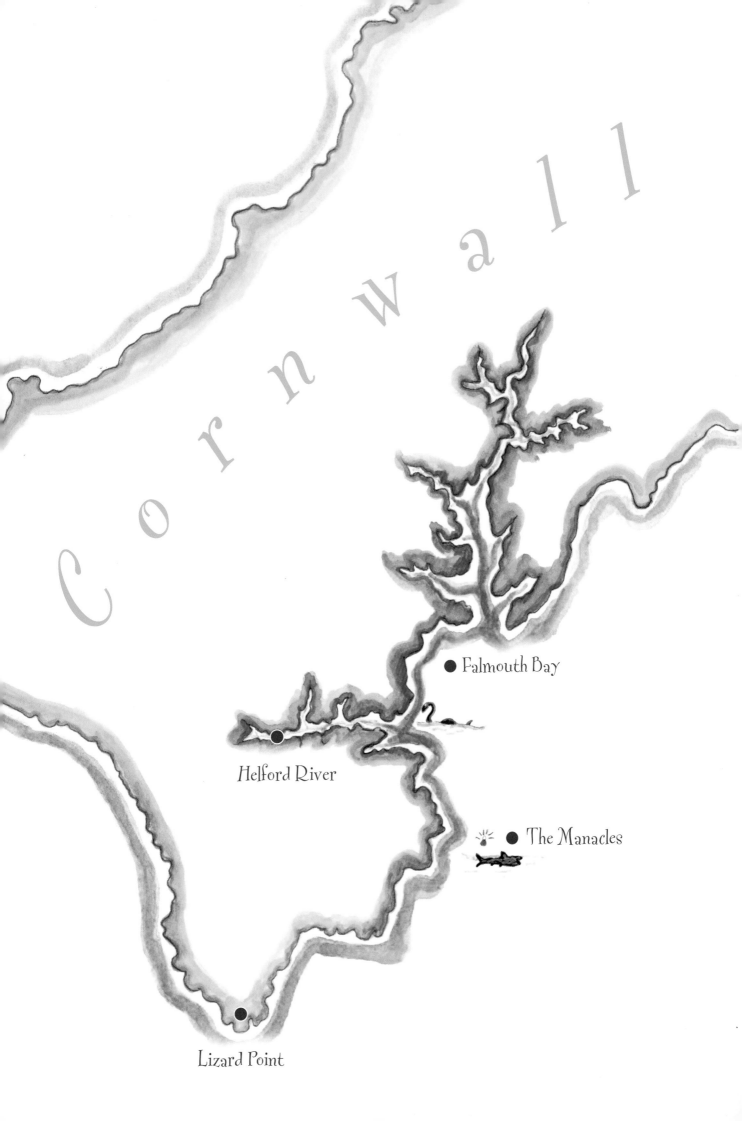

Cornwall

● Falmouth Bay

● Helford River

The Manacles

● Lizard Point

How many of you noticed
that the planet on page 10
was drawn as it is today
and not as it was then?

The land of Pangaea
broke away in several bits.
Our world in Cretaceouse times
looked, I hope, like this!